THE 12 WORST
HUMAN-MADE
DISASTERS OF ALL TIME

by Susan E. Hamen

www.12StoryLibrary.com

12-Story Library is an imprint of Bookstaves.

Photographs ©:US Coast Guard, cover, 1; TK/Associated Press, 4; DS/Associated Press, 5; US Geological Survey, 5; Tormod Sandtorv/CC2.0, 6; flydime/CC3.0, 7; baselactionnetwork/CC2.0, 8; baselactionnetwork/CC2.0, 9; Joshua Stevens/NASA, 10; serkan senturk/Shutterstock.com, 11; NASA Earth Observatory, 12; Arian Zwegers/CC2.0, 13; stahlmandesign/CC2.0, 14; Roman Harak/CC2.0, 15; Délmagyarország/Karnok Csaba/CC3.0, 16; Calin Stan/Shutterstock.com, 17; Xinhua/Chi Haifeng/Associated Press, 18; CHINATOPIX/Associated Press, 19; Julian Nitzsche/CC3.0, 20; Sondeep Shankar/Associated Press, 21; Rich Carey/Shutterstock.com, 22; MOHAMED ABDULRAHEEM/Shutterstock.com, 23; US Coast Guard, 24; NOAA's National Ocean Service, 25; Greg Webb/IAEA/CC2.0, 26; Nishi81/Shutterstock.com, 27; Ekaterina_Minaeva/Shutterstock.com, 28; photka/Shutterstock.com, 29

ISBN
978-1-63235-539-3 (hardcover)
978-1-63235-604-8 (paperback)
978-1-63235-658-1 (ebook)

Library of Congress Control Number: 2018946709

Printed in the United States of America
Mankato, MN
June 2018

About the Cover
Deepwater Horizon oil rig on fire, April 20, 2010.

Access free, up-to-date content on this topic plus a full digital version of this book. Scan the QR code on page 31 or use your school's login at 12StoryLibrary.com.

Table of Contents

Toxic Sludge Poisons New York State Neighborhood

In the 1970s, children in the Love Canal neighborhood of Niagara Falls, New York, started getting sick. Some developed diseases such as epilepsy and asthma. Many babies were born premature. Others had birth defects. A number of children never grew their adult teeth. When black goo began seeping up from the grass, residents knew something was wrong.

One young mother took action. Lois Gibbs had two children who were sick. She read a newspaper article that said chemical waste was buried in the area. Lois spoke to her neighbors. She recorded the conditions residents had. Her work gained national attention.

Officials began to investigate. They found that the Hooker

Love Canal neighborhood.

The foundation of a home that was relocated. Behind is the filled-in chemical dump.

Children protest at a neighborhood rally in 1978.

Chemical Company had dumped chemical waste in Love Canal decades earlier. The site was later covered with clay. It was then sold to the city. A school was built on the site.

Over time, chemicals ate through the clay. They seeped up out of the ground. Children spent their recess on a playground with black, mucky, toxic goop. These poisonous chemicals made Love Canal residents sick.

56

Percent of children in Love Canal born with birth defects from 1974 to 1978.

- Children in Love Canal began getting sick in the 1970s.
- Toxic chemicals had been buried in the area.
- Exposure to the chemicals caused birth defects and diseases.

A PREVENTABLE DISASTER

The Hooker Chemical Company told city officials about the buried chemicals. But officials didn't pass along warnings to people who bought homes in the Love Canal neighborhood. The state of New York eventually purchased the homes of nearly 1,000 families in the area. It also paid to relocate people.

5

"Door to Hell" Burns for Decades in Turkmenistan Desert

Geologists went to the Karakum Desert in 1971 to find oil. They began to drill in present-day Turkmenistan near the village of Darvaza. These scientists did not find oil. Instead, they drilled right into a large pocket of natural gas.

When oil drills hit the natural gas cavity, the ground gave way. It couldn't support the weight of the machinery. The entire site collapsed. Other areas near the drill site also caved in. Open craters dotted the Karakum Desert.

The large craters gave off natural gas. It contained a gas called methane. The methane made it difficult for people and animals to breathe. Scientists noticed desert animals dying. Something had to be done.

Geologists lit the natural gas field on fire. They hoped the gas would burn off quickly. After a few weeks, the fires still burned. Months passed. Then years. Then decades.

More than 40 years later, the Darvaza gas crater is still on fire.

The crater is 225 feet (69 m) across. Many people call it the "Door to Hell."

In 2010, the president of Turkmenistan ordered the crater to be filled in. He believed this would allow geologists to drill for oil in nearby areas. But officials have yet to take action. The crater has become a tourist attraction. No one knows how long the fire will burn.

99
Depth in feet (30 m) of the burning crater.

- The Darvaza Gas Crater was created by geologists drilling for oil.
- Scientists lit a fire in the crater to burn off natural gas containing methane.
- The crater has been burning for more than 40 years.

E-Waste Harms Environment in Chinese Town

In Guiyu, China, people make their living on junk. That's because the town receives large shipments of electronic waste from around the globe.

The people of Guiyu break down old computers, printers, cell phones, and other electronics. They recycle as many parts as they can. Until recently, they did almost all of their work by hand. They piled wires and plastic pieces in the streets. They used their hands to stir circuitry in chemicals to clean them. They burned other parts over open fires. The fires released poisonous gases into the air. The air smelled like acid.

Researchers found that the groundwater wasn't safe to drink. Mercury from flat-screen monitors was poisoning streams and fish. Children had high levels of lead in their blood. Lead can

People sort through wires torn out of computers.

Plastic encased parts are burned to reduce them to metals.

THINK ABOUT IT

What are some ways people can reduce the amount of electronic waste in the environment? How might you and your family create less e-waste?

affect intelligence and the central nervous system. Organizations like Greenpeace worked to stop the shipment of e-waste to Guiyu. But people there worried they would not be able to support their families.

In the early 2010s, the local government decided to clean up the town. They cracked down on family recycling workshops. They opened an industrial park that made recycling safer. Workers earn less money today, but the town is cleaner. In early 2018, the Chinese government banned some types of foreign trash.

70
Percent of the world's e-waste sent to China in 2013.

- Workers in Guiyu take apart electronics to recycle valuable materials.
- Electronics contain toxic chemicals.
- Children in Guiyu had high levels of lead in their bodies from the e-waste.
- The Chinese government has banned some types of foreign trash.

4

Sulfur Dioxide Sickens Iraqis Near Mosul

On June 24, 2003, a fire broke out at the Al-Mishraq sulfur plant near Mosul, Iraq. Sulfur is used to make batteries, detergents, and other products. In large quantities, it pollutes the environment.

Officials believe arsonists set fire to the sulfur plant. It caused a major disaster. The blaze burned for nearly a month. Nearly 600,000 metric tons of sulfur dioxide were released into the air. That is more than most big volcanic eruptions produce. The fire also released toxic hydrogen sulfide.

The poisons in the air devastated the area. Vegetation near the plant died. Nearly $40 million in crops were destroyed. People living in the area had respiratory illnesses. They struggled to breathe. Two people died. By the time it was put out, the Al-Mishraq fire was the largest human-caused release of sulfur dioxide in history.

Tigris River

Al-Mishraq sulfur plant

Qayyarah oil field

Sulfur plume

Oil plume

A SECOND FIRE DOES MORE DAMAGE

In 2016, the Al-Mishraq sulfur plant was started on fire again. This time, it was militants fighting for control of Mosul. The blaze did not last as long as the 2003 fire. It was put out within seven days. But it still released large amounts of sulfur dioxide. Up to 1,000 Iraqis were treated for breathing problems. Two more people died.

$20 million
Amount of sulfur lost in the fire.

- Arsonists started a fire at the Al-Mishraq sulfur plant in 2003.
- The fire sent about 600,000 metric tons of sulfur dioxide into the air.
- Al-Mishraq is the largest ever human-caused release of polluting sulfur dioxide.

The smoke caused respiratory problems.

11

Irrigation Shrinks Asia's Aral Sea

The Aral Sea in Asia is not really a sea. It has fresh water, not salt water. It is inland, in what used to be part of the Soviet Union. So the Aral Sea is a lake. It was once the fourth-largest lake in the world. Water from nearby mountains flowed to it from two major rivers. The rivers are the Amu Darya and the Syr Darya.

In 1918, the Soviet government decided to grow crops on land surrounding the Aral Sea. But the land was very dry. So they started a huge irrigation project. Engineers built 20,000 miles (32,187 km) of canals. They built 45 dams and more than 80 reservoirs. Water from the Amu Darya and the Syr Darya was diverted. Instead of flowing into the Aral Sea, it went to millions of acres of cotton and wheat.

The image on the left shows the Aral Sea in 2014. The one on the right is from 2000.

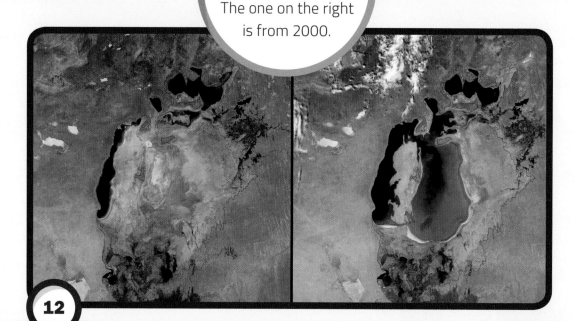

Boats were abandoned after the fishing industry was destroyed.

The Aral Sea started to shrink. Over time, it shrank to one-tenth its original size. Millions of fish died. The area's fishing industry was destroyed. People had to leave to find new jobs. Towns along the shoreline of the lake grew smaller. People who stayed faced bad dust storms. Winds blew up dust from the dried-up areas of the lake. The dust was filled with chemicals and pesticides from the crops.

Efforts are underway to bring water back to the Aral Sea. But it is unlikely the lake will ever return to its original size.

26,000
The Aral Sea's surface area before 1960, in square miles (67,340 sq km).

- Soviet engineers diverted rivers feeding the Aral Sea.
- Over time, the Aral Sea was reduced to one-tenth its original size.
- The fishing industry was destroyed, forcing many people to move.

6

Nuclear Disaster Creates a Ghost Town in Ukraine

Pripyat was once a thriving young city in the Soviet Union. Today it is a ghost town in northern Ukraine. Founded in 1970, Pripyat was built on nuclear power. Most people who lived there worked at the nearby Chernobyl nuclear power plant. On April 26, 1986, everything changed.

Aerial view of the explosion.

The trouble began when workers at Chernobyl prepared to test the plant's nuclear systems. They disabled automatic shutdowns. These were meant to limit damage if things went wrong. During testing, a large explosion occurred. With automatic shutdowns turned off, workers couldn't stop a second explosion. A large mushroom cloud of smoke and steam rose into the sky. Fires blazed inside the plant.

The Chernobyl accident was the largest uncontrolled radioactive release in history. Radioactive material blew as far as Scandinavia. Explosions at the plant killed two

АВАРІЯ НА 4-МУ БЛОЦІ ЧАЕС
ACCIDENT AT CHNPP UNIT 4

An abandoned school in Pripyat.

workers. Another 28 people later died from radiation exposure.

The government evacuated people living within 20 miles (32 km) of the plant. Many would never return. No one went back to Pripyat. Radiation made it too dangerous. Apartment buildings remain standing. Schools, too. Roads still run through the city. Communist propaganda hangs on walls. But there are no people. It won't be safe to live in Pripyat again for thousands of years.

336,000
Total number of people evacuated after the Chernobyl accident.

- Pripyat was a busy city, home to many workers at the Chernobyl plant.
- Two explosions occurred at the Chernobyl nuclear site in 1986.
- Radiation makes it unsafe for people to live near the disaster site.

WHAT IS NUCLEAR ENERGY?

All things are made of tiny particles called atoms. When atoms are broken apart, nuclear energy is released. This energy can be used to create electric power. Uranium atoms release large amounts of energy when broken apart. However, uranium is radioactive. That means it can hurt people if is not used safely.

Cyanide Spill in Romania Is Environmental Catastrophe

Gold is produced in the city of Baia Mare, Romania. First, rocks from a nearby mine are smashed into dust. Then the dust is mixed with water. Cyanide is added to the water. The cyanide pulls the gold from the rock dust. It is very poisonous.

The gold processing plant in Baia Mare stored cyanide-infected water in two human-made lakes. The pollutants were meant to never get out. But on January 30, 2000, a disastrous accident happened. A dam burst. About 34 million gallons of cyanide-tainted water were released. The water flowed into the Lupes, Somes, Tisza, and Danube rivers.

Following the spill, some parts of the rivers lost all of their fish. The water was unsafe for humans. But people did not know that. They drank water from the rivers. They ate fish from the rivers. Within a year, clinics in Baia Mare were filled with people sick from cyanide. They had respiratory problems and digestive conditions. All were made sick from the spill.

100

Number of people hospitalized after eating contaminated fish from affected rivers.

- A water and cyanide solution was used to extract gold in Romania.
- In 2000, a dam burst, releasing cyanide-tainted water into four rivers.
- Cyanide killed fish and made the water unsafe for humans to drink.

A POISONED FOOD CHAIN

Fish were not the only wildlife affected by the cyanide spill. Other wild animals also died. When fish killed by the cyanide came to rest on shore, other animals ate them. Many foxes, ospreys, river otters, and birds died after eating poisoned fish.

Chemical Explosion in China Forces Evacuation

The Number 101 chemical plant in China was the first of its kind. It was a large facility producing chemicals to make plastic. The plant was located in China's northeast province of Jilin. In November 2005, something terrible happened at the Number 101 plant.

Around noon on November 13, a tower in the benzene production area became blocked. A plant employee tried to unblock it. He couldn't. There was a large explosion. The blast shattered windows in buildings more than 600 feet (183 m) away. More explosions followed. A fire also erupted in the plant. It took 300 firefighters to extinguish the blaze.

The explosions released nearly 100 tons of pollutants. Benzene and nitrobenzene poured into the Songhua River. Toxic sludge floated on the surface of the water. Jilin City was forced to evacuate 42,000 people. Tests showed benzene

Smoke from the explosion could be seen for miles.

levels in Jilin City rose to 108 times the safety level. Benzene exposure can cause leukemia and other diseases.

Following the accident, the water supply was shut off to stop the spread of contamination. For a time, tens of millions of people were without water. But it was to keep them from getting sick.

The benzene spill was an international incident. The Songhua River joins the Amur

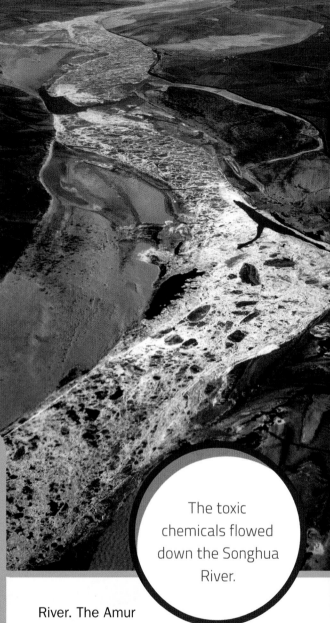

50

Length of toxic sludge slick in miles (80 km).

- A series of explosions released benzene in Jilin, China.
- Tens of thousands of people were evacuated from the area.
- Tens of millions of people were left without access to clean water.
- China apologized to Russia for the benzene spill.

The toxic chemicals flowed down the Songhua River.

River. The Amur forms the border between Northeastern China and Russia's Far East. Then it flows into Russia. China apologized to Russia for the spill.

Toxic Gas Leak Is India's Worst Industrial Accident

It was a chilly evening in December 1984. People in Bhopal, India, had settled down to sleep. They could not know they would awake to a nightmare.

Overnight, a worker at the Union Carbide pesticide plant noticed a leak of toxic gases. A faulty valve later allowed a ton of water to mix with 40 tons of the gases. This caused a reaction.

500,000
Estimated number of people left with respiratory problems and other health conditions.

- The Union Carbide accident released toxic gases into the air.
- Hundreds of thousands of people were exposed to the poisonous gas.
- Many survivors have experienced ongoing health problems.

The pesticide plant that released the toxic gases.

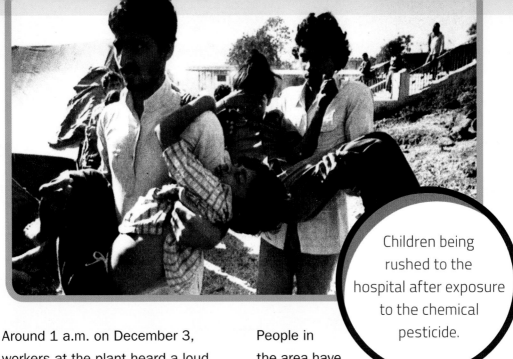

Children being rushed to the hospital after exposure to the chemical pesticide.

Around 1 a.m. on December 3, workers at the plant heard a loud rumbling sound. A cloud of toxic gases shot into the air above the plant. Then the cloud sank close to the ground. It covered the city of Bhopal.

Nearly 600,000 people were directly exposed to the chemical cloud. Almost immediately, people died from the poisonous gas. Up to 20,000 people lost their lives. Those who survived struggled to breathe. The gas burned their throats and eyes. Many were permanently blinded.

The site remains contaminated. It was not cleaned after the disaster.

People in the area have had ongoing health problems. Survivors' children have been born with disabilities. The Union Carbide chemical leak is the worst industrial accident in the history of India.

THINK ABOUT IT

Why do you think the accident site was never cleaned up? How was the company able to get out of that responsibility? Research online to learn more.

Huge Floating Garbage Patch Threatens Marine Life

There is a lot of garbage in the world's oceans. People on shore drop plastic bottles, bags, and other items into the water. Other trash comes from boats and oil rigs.

The litter rides on ocean currents. In the Pacific Ocean, it is carried to one of two growing patches of garbage. One patch is off the shore of Japan. The other lies between the US states

1.8 trillion

Estimated number of pieces of plastic floating in the garbage patch.

- Litter dropped into the Pacific Ocean floats to garbage patches.
- Much of the trash in garbage patches is plastic.
- Many marine animals die from eating plastic in the ocean.

GHOST NETTING

Discarded fishing nets make up nearly half of the trash in the garbage patch. These are called "ghost nets." Sea turtles, lobsters, whales, sharks, and other animals get caught in the nets and die. The nets are made of materials that can last up to 600 years. Conservation groups are trying to clean up the 640,000 tons of abandoned nets and fishing gear in the world's oceans.

of Hawaii and California. Debris in garbage patches swirls in a circle.

Much of the trash in garbage patches is made from plastic. It doesn't biodegrade or disappear. It simply breaks into smaller pieces over time. This waste is harmful to marine life. Sea turtles choke on plastic bags. They mistake bags for their favorite food, jellyfish. To albatrosses, plastic pieces look like fish eggs. They feed them to chicks, causing them to die.

The two garbage patches in the Pacific Ocean make up what is called the Great Pacific Garbage Patch. Scientists estimate that its total area is twice the size of the US state of Texas.

Gulf Oil Spill Is Worst in US History

On April 20, 2010, workers on the Deepwater Horizon oil rig prepared to celebrate. The oil rig floated in the Gulf of Mexico. Seven years had passed without a serious accident. There was another reason to celebrate. Workers had finished drilling a well 13,000 feet (3,962 m)

126

Number of workers on the Deepwater Horizon at time of blast.

- An accident on the Deepwater Horizon oil rig caused a massive oil spill.
- It took 87 days to stop the flow of oil into the Gulf of Mexico.
- Hundreds of thousands of animals were killed.

A veterinarian prepares to clean an oiled turtle after the spill.

beneath the ocean floor. They were finally ready to start pumping oil and gas from the well.

Suddenly a surge of natural gas burst through a concrete core designed to seal the well. The gas traveled up to the rig and lit on fire. The blast killed 11 workers. The huge rig eventually capsized and sank.

Oil flowed from the well below the sunken oil rig. It took emergency workers 87 days to cap the well and stop the stream of oil. By that time, 206 million gallons of oil had flowed into the Gulf of Mexico.

Scientists estimate that oil slicks killed 800,000 brown pelicans and 65,000 sea turtles. Fish, dolphins, and whales in the area were also affected. Large numbers of mutated fish appeared after the accident. Deformed fish are still found today.

THINK ABOUT IT

Many people are opposed to offshore oil drilling. They believe the risk of spills is too high. Do you think oil should be drilled offshore? Why or why not?

Earthquake Leads to Nuclear Meltdown in Japan

An earthquake hit Japan on March 11, 2011. That was the first of many catastrophic events. Within an hour, tsunami waves battered Japan's coastline. Walls of water up to 128 feet high (39 m) traveled six miles (9.6 km) inland.

One of those waves hit the Fukushima Daiichi nuclear power plant. The emergency power generators in the plant's basement flooded. This caused cooling systems to stop working. Soon, fuel rods in the nuclear reactor at the plant began to melt. Deadly radiation leaked out. Within hours, fuel rods in another two reactors melted down.

The government of Japan waited 88 days before admitting that a nuclear meltdown had happened at Fukushima. By that time, radioactive water had seeped into the ocean and surrounding soil.

After the meltdown, a wall was built around the damaged plant to keep more radioactive water from escaping. Contaminated topsoil was collected for later disposal. This cleanup continues today. It may take up to 40 years to get rid of all the radioactive waste.

Inspection of Reactor Unit 3 after the disaster.

Disposal of the contaminated topsoil from the disaster area has been controversial.

800,000
Tons of radioactive water being held at the plant and awaiting disposal.

- An earthquake caused a tsunami that hit the Fukushima Daiichi nuclear power plant.
- Three nuclear reactors melted down, releasing radiation into the environment.
- It may take up to 40 years to completely clean up the radioactive waste.

About 2,000 people died as a result of the Fukushima disaster. These deaths could have been prevented. Workers at the plant had tried to warn management about old pipes and poor wall construction. Many felt the nuclear meltdown might have been prevented if the plant had addressed these issues. The Fukushima Daiichi nuclear plant meltdown is the second-worst nuclear disaster in the history of the world.

Staying Safe If There Is a Human-Made Disaster

- Work with your family to make a disaster plan. Know where the safe spots are in every room of your home.

- Establish a meeting place away from home where family members can meet in case of an evacuation.

- Keep copies of important documents such as birth certificates, passports, insurance papers, and a list of bank accounts together in a waterproof bag that is easy to grab quickly. Also include some cash.

- Stock up on essential supplies, such as canned food, granola bars, peanut butter, dried fruit, and bottled water.

Family Disaster Plan and

IV. IF YOU EVACUATE

Take with you:

- Medicines and first aid kit
- Flashlight, radio and batteries
- Important documents and cash
- Blankets and extra clothes
- Personal sanitary items
- Any additional items you f...

- If a known outbreak or epidemic reaches your community, cover your mouth and nose with a surgical mask when you have to go out in public.

- Establish healthy habits, such as frequent handwashing. Cover your mouth and nose when you cough or sneeze to prevent the spread of illness.

- Keep the names and numbers of family doctors, clinics, and pharmacies up to date and easy to find. Keep an up-to-date list of health information like allergies, medical conditions, and blood type.

- If you require daily medication, make sure you have a supply on hand in case you are unable to leave your home.

Glossary

arsonist
A person who intentionally sets something on fire.

benzene
A colorless, flammable chemical used in the production of plastics.

cyanide
A poisonous salt that is often used to extract gold or silver from rock.

dam
A barrier that is built to hold back water.

epilepsy
A brain disorder that causes seizures or periods of unusual behavior.

methane
A colorless and odorless gas that provides energy.

nuclear reactor
A piece of equipment that produces nuclear energy.

oil slick
A film or layer of oil floating on the surface of the water.

pesticide
A chemical or other substance used to kill insects.

radiation
The transmission of energy in the form of waves or particles.

radioactive
Something that gives off energy in the form of waves or particles.

tsunami
A long ocean wave caused by an earthquake that can cause massive destruction on land.

For More Information

Books

Dickmann, Nancy. *Energy from Nuclear Fission: Splitting the Atom.* Next Generation Energy. New York: Crabtree Publishing, 2015.

Perdew, Laura. *The Great Pacific Garbage Patch.* Ecological Disasters. Minneapolis, MN: Abdo Publishing, 2017.

Stone, Adam. *The Deepwater Horizon Oil Spill.* Minnetonka, MN: Bellwether Media, 2016.

Visit 12StoryLibrary.com

Scan the code or use your school's login at **12StoryLibrary.com** for recent updates about this topic and a full digital version of this book. Enjoy free access to:

- Digital ebook
- Breaking news updates
- Live content feeds
- Videos, interactive maps, and graphics
- Additional web resources

Note to educators: Visit 12StoryLibrary.com/register to sign up for free premium website access. Enjoy live content plus a full digital version of every 12-Story Library book you own for every student at your school.

Index

About the Author

Susan E. Hamen has written more than 30 books for children on various topics, including the Wright brothers, World War II, and ancient Rome. Hamen lives in Minnesota with her husband, daughter, and son.